SHOP on WHEELS

SHOP on WHEELS

A bicycle, trailer & searchlight battery

A WARTIME DIARY, SUFFOLK 1942-44

M. Janet Becker

Edited by Alan Mackley

BLYTHBURGH BOOKS

First published in 2024
by
BLYTHBURGH BOOKS
1 Angel Lane
Blythburgh
Halesworth
Suffolk
IP19 9LU

Email bburghbooks@btinternet.com

ISBN 978-1-912427-23-9

Proceeds from the sale of this book will be donated to
Holy Trinity Church, Blythburgh, and a leukaemia charity

Typeset in Colibri Light and Baskerville

Cover and title designs by Jeff Fisher

Printed and bound by

Southwold Press Ltd

www.southwoldpress.co.uk

01502 7233361

Editing the diary

For consistency and clarity, spelling has been corrected, abbreviations expanded, and capitalisation, punctuation and underlining modified. Deleted words have been ignored. Editorial additions are shown in square brackets.

Acknowledgements

Thanks are due to Simon Loftus, from whose collection of Becker papers this diary emerged, and Jeff Taylor of the Suffolk Book League, whose enquiry reignited my interest in Janet Becker. Those who have helped to answer questions include Steve Bell and Robert Collis, Norfolk and Suffolk Aviation Museum; Fiona Cairns, Suffolk Preservation Society; Tony Copsey, Suffolk Artists website; Meryl Doney and Sue Powell, Friends of Blythburgh Holy Trinity Church; Fran D'Alcorn, St Felix School; John English, Walberswick Local History Society; David Jacobs, Jewish Historical Society of England; Professor Robert Liddiard, University of East Anglia; Edward Waddington; Robert Winckworth, University College London Records, and the Department of Theatre and Performance, Victoria and Albert Museum. Jeff Fisher produced fine designs for the cover and titles, and Mike Durrant for the map.

Financial support from the Sizewell Community Fund and the Scarfe Trust is gratefully acknowledged.

Alan Mackley
Blythburgh
2024

Janet Becker in 1950. (© Simon Loftus)

Introduction

From December 1942 to October 1944, Janet Becker, a single woman in her early forties, living with her widowed mother in the small east Suffolk village of Wangford, kept an occasional diary. It describes the support she gave to a Royal Artillery searchlight unit in Henham Park.[1] She cycled no fewer than 175 times the $1\frac{1}{2}$ miles from her home, towing a trailer behind her – her 'Shop on Wheels'. She supplied necessities of life such as razor blades, toothpaste, hair-cream and Mars bars. There were also treats like hot buns, and she collected and returned uniforms and socks that the ladies of Wangford had sewn and darned.

Wangford, 3 miles (5 km) from the North Sea coast, was deep inside the Suffolk Sandlings, an area described by Liddiard and Sims as 'A Very Dangerous Locality' in the Second World War.[2] Some of the area was given over to battle training with live ammunition. Early in the war the Suffolk coast was thought vulnerable to invasion. When that threat receded, it remained in the front line of defence against enemy bombers. The searchlight at Henham was one of a network of sites spaced every ten km or so apart. Allied aircraft provided an additional hazard and the troops found themselves dealing with all-too frequent disasters involving friendly planes.

Janet Becker was born in London in 1903. In 1913 she had come to live in the Suffolk village of Wenhaston with her artist father Harry Becker, and her mother Georgina. They spent a short

---

[1] Henham Hall, surrounded by a 500-acre park, was the seat of the earl of Stradbroke. The park is best known in the twenty-first century as the location of the Latitude Festival. The hall was used by the army during the war. The searchlight battery site has Suffolk Historical Environment Monument Record No. WNF 045, centred on map reference TM 4562 7786.

[2] Robert Liddiard and David Sims, *A Very Dangerous Locality. The Landscape of the Suffolk Sandlings in the Second World* War (2018), Figure 4.11. p.148, shows the distribution of searchlight sites in east Suffolk in 1942. The Henham site was manned initially by a detachment of 329 Battery of 32 Searchlight Regiment, Royal Artillery, and from 1942 by their 320 Searchlight Battery.

time in Hinton, a hamlet of Blythburgh, before her father died in 1928. Janet was a pioneer woman professional cleaner and restorer of church monuments. From the early 1930s she travelled widely but her heart was always in east Suffolk. After her first book on the medieval accounts of Rochester Bridge was published, everything Janet Becker wrote, whether historical studies, fiction or poetry, was rooted in the area.[3] Her career was on hold during the war. But her diary shows how much her personal interests determined the support she gave to the servicemen. A lecture in a barrack hut, a demonstration of wood-block printing, writing love poems for soldiers to send to girl-friends and wives, the making of Valentines – her interests and also her determination show through.

The general tone of the diary is light-hearted and Janet's literary sense and love of the landscape is clear. Shrapnel flying from an exploding plane does not simply strike the earth, it lands in flowers and leaves. Tragedy was never far away. Janet reflected for example that 'she had begun this book on the lighter side' when she felt she should include an account of someone learning that his mother had died.

Janet's work was appreciated. The Major came up to her one day as she left the camp: 'Miss Becker? I've heard so much about you from the men and seen your name up on notices about mending socks, and I'm delighted to have this opportunity of thanking you personally for all you're doing.' She was assured that she was never in the way, and in the village shop one of the men volunteered: 'My word, Miss Becker's a good sort - you don't know all she does for us.'

The diary is a charming contemporary source that describes military-civilian relations during the Second World War.

After the war Janet Becker resumed her work on church monuments. She died from leukaemia in 1953.

---

[3] Janet Becker published two historical studies, two novels, a volume of verse and some shorter works.

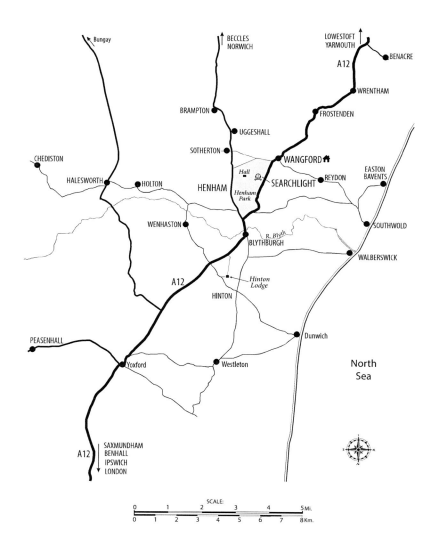

Part of north-east Suffolk, indicating PLACES
MENTIONED IN TEXT and other locations.

A Royal Artillery anti-aircraft searchlight and crew at the Royal Hospital Chelsea, London, 17 April 1940. (© Imperial War Museum H 1291)

The Diary
SHOP ON WHEELS

30th December, 1942.

When I was a child the two occupations most delightful to me were pushing an object on wheels and keeping shop. So then, how satisfying is my pleasure, when, within a few months of my 40th birthday, I find myself in charge of a little mobile canteen for the local searchlight unit.

After a wild night of wind and sleet I set out to push the canteen a mile out of the village along the main road covered with slush. Arrived at the camp I hailed the first man I saw (S.W. Smith) who happened to be in the guard room and he came out and inhaled the aroma of the still-hot buns, and adjusted the catch of the door for me. As I pushed the canteen up the slope into the main part of the camp the sentry behind his sandbag wall had his back to me, but he turned round and I waved to him. It was H.W. Reynolds, and he came across the snowy ground, tilting his tin hat. Ace, the sergeant's dog, came out from under a hut like Peter Rabbit squeezing under Mr McGregor's gate[4] - and escorted me along the line of huts while the sentry walked on the other side of the barbed wire between us, coming off duty. I asked him if the noises in the night above the storm had been, as I thought, mines exploding on the coast. We credit the Searchlight men with knowing everything. 'So that's what they were' he explained. 'We wondered.'

In the cookhouse, Bailes, the officer's batman was warming himself. 'Easy time for you' I said, knowing the latter was on

---

[4] An image from Beatrix Potter, *The Tale of Peter Rabbit* (1902).

leave. 'Oh,' said Bailes, whose life as a post office sorter with a weak wrist has been sadly shaken up by the war, 'I'm on 48 hrs sick leave – inoculation.' 'What against?' I enquired, 'Depression?' sitting down to the proffered cup of tea, and he actually laughed. Boyd sat opposite me, peeling potatoes, dipping his wrists luxuriantly into hot water to fetch up those from the bottom of the pail. The cookhouse began to fill up. Reynolds came in 'to thaw out' as he put it, blowing on his nails, in spite of his leather clothing. I was reminded of recorded scenes in a monastic 'calefactory' or warm room, where the monks were allowed so often a day to get warm. [5] Really, these men are living parallel lives with the monks – living removed from homes and families, on constant duty in the service of that grim gun and the searchlight, screened by the belt of ancient trees encircling the parkland … The senior cook has made the tea by emptying several handfuls of tea and a tin of condensed milk into a bucket, and poured over it the contents of a can of water off the stove. From everywhere men came running up like rabbits – from under camouflage netting, out of huts, from behind artificial walls; running up like rabbits, white tuffs pressed against their khaki bodies (their tea mugs). I have finished my own cup. I go out and stand by the canteen in the icy wind on the muddy track. They all crowd round me. Today I have to sell the two things in life worth buying, razor blades and Mars bars – or is it Mars bars and razor blades?

6th January, 1943.

A sprinkling of snow. An air of tension in the camp, an inspection pending. Boyd, coming out of the cookhouse as the canteen approached, let out a yell announcing tea, saw me and stopped short. He and Shambrook in spotless white duck and their regular cookhouse footwear - clogs. The cookhouse newly

---

[5] Calefactory or Warming Room in a medieval monastery, where monks could warm themselves after periods in the cold, studying or working.

swilled down, and a brand-new roller towel hung up in preparation for the officer's visit.[6]

I took up a bottle of ginger wine labelled 'Reserved for Sentries in the Snow' and Sergeant Goddard, sitting on the kitchen table, said there would be a rush of volunteers that night, and he proposed taking a guard himself.

16th January, 1943.

Sergeant Goddard told me when he goes into Battery at Saxmundham men gather round him and ask where he gets that 'Brylcream shine' and that he replies 'We have a very good mobile canteen service.'[7]

20th January, 1943.

Ace lying cuddled in Bailes' arms over the fire – hind legs and tail supported by one arm, front paws upheld by the other, head resting on the batman's shoulder. Boyd: 'He's missing the old man dreadful' (Sergeant Podger, on 7 days leave).

23rd January, 1943.

A Home Guard was in the cookhouse, and there was much chaff between him and Sergeants Goddard and Sinclair about a proposed shooting match. It appeared the Home Guard ammunition didn't fit their rifles, and he said they couldn't use any other rifles because the sights would be wrong.[8] Sergeant Sinclair apologised for talking so much 'shop' as I got up to go; I said 'That's all right. All I ask is that you take care of yourselves,'

---

[6] The chain of command in the Royal Artillery was: Regiment>Battery>Troop.

[7] A heavily-promoted and popular hair cream, associated especially with RAF air-crew: 'The Brylcream Boys.'

[8] The Home Guard was issued with American M1917 Enfield rifles, using a 0.3 inch round, different from (and more powerful than) the .303 round used in the service issue Lee-Enfield rifles.

meaning I thought it was brave of them to shoot with the Home Guard!

As I was talking to Bombardier Bachelor a man came out of the recreation hut and told him 'Porter' was out of cigarettes.[9] Batchelor thereupon let out a yell which went ringing round the park and echoed back to us, 'Porter, Porter.' A head appeared at the door of a distant hut. 'I can't come. I'm on duty here.' 'Come here' ordered Batchelor, so the man got his cigarettes.

27th January, 1943.

Shambrook feeling sore, figuratively and literally, having been vaccinated. 'They'll be sending us out East, next, and I shan't half dislike sand in my soups.'

30th January, 1943.

A discussion with Sergeant Podger in the cookhouse on the recognition of aircraft. Shambrook chimed in. 'I know what they all are, Miss Becker – they're all just aeroplanes to me.'

I took Tommy Wincop with me to present a pair of gloves he had knitted, to the winner of the draw I arranged. They were all very nice to him and took him into the recreation hut for the little ceremony. When I joined them after my trading the winner (a man I didn't know, L.J. Reynolds) was just receiving them. Sergeant Podger made Tommy a little speech, saying when <u>he</u> was in the army they'd try and knit for him, only their beards and whiskers would probably get in the way. Sergeant Podger escorted us to the gate – 'I don't often see you' he said!

3rd February, 1943.

All the men keen on Valentines I was making to augment the Comforts Fund. I took up a notice for the recreation hut, at which all in the cookhouse looked. Sergeant Podger twitted

---

[9] Bombardier, a rank in the Royal Artillery, equivalent to corporal in other arms.

Shambrook (married) with wanting to buy one. He retorted with perfect simplicity and probable truth 'My wife can still be my sweetheart can't she?'

I also took a knitted chicken Pam Freeman made to sell to Sergeant Goddard for his baby. Everyone who came in had to be shown it – 'Come and see what I've got for my baby.'

21st February, 1943.

I went up on Sunday because of the Town and Country Conference on Saturday at Ipswich.[10] Being Sunday (I suppose) the cookhouse was full – three sergeants, a Home Guard sergeant, the two cooks, Bailes, Banham (vainly trying to collect money for newspapers from Sergeant Podger who said he'd paid, while Sergeant Burgess claimed the paper as his), myself and a man who'd come for his tea, and, of course, Ace.

27th February, 1943.

This morning just before I started, a message from the officer, could I in future come up at 10.30 instead of 11, as the 'break' was altered to the former time. When the sergeants asked me if it made any difference to me, I said none, but that in future they would have to do without their new buns. 'What, do without our new buns! Then break will be at 11 on Wednesdays and Saturdays.'

I said I supposed they would fix it with the officer. 'Oh, we'll tell John break is at 11 on those days just to keep him in touch with things.' Sergeant Burgess is rather shy and easily blushes – so is heavily teased on that account. Looking out of the window he drew my attention to the newly whitened tops of the

---

[10] The issue was highly topical. The conference passed unanimously the resolution: 'That this conference representing local government bodies in East Anglia and others interested in town and country planning calls upon the Government to expedite its declaration of policy in regard to planning, so that local authorities may know what they are expected to do in the future.' The Ministry of Town and Country Planning was formed in 1943 and 'The Town and Country Planning (Interim Development) Act, 1943' received Royal Assent on 22 July 1943.

posts lining the paths. Sergeant Goddard said 'We must ask Miss Becker to have a turn at our coconut shy.' 'What's the prize?' I asked. 'Sergeant Burgess' replied Sergeant Goddard to the pitiful confusion of Sergeant Burgess.

3rd March, 1943.

The bustle in the camp still persisted from Sunday. I walked up that day with onions and found everyone dashing about changing over huts and spring cleaning. Bailes came dashing along carrying water in a leaking can – it was a race between the water and himself. Outside the store hut were $16\frac{1}{2}$ pairs of Wellington boots and in the cookhouse dozens of kippers. One of the men had brought a supply from Yarmouth, only to find a similar amount had been issued with the rations. All this activity was due to the imminent inspection by the Brigadier the coming Thursday.

So today Wednesday, the activity had reached fever pitch with colour washing. One man, Howlett, came out of a hut covered from head to foot with it, having had a tin dropped over him from a ladder. Sergeant Podger came along rolling the camp canteen's barrel of beer. The Major was arriving any minute to give them a rehearsal for the morrow, and it was not supposed to be the thing to have beer on the sites. Sergeant Podger went further and further across the park, and every dip, depression or gorse bush he tried to hide it in, it seemed to grow bigger and to stick out more! Finally he rolled it into a ditch with a sigh of relief, and returned from his one-man act of Rolling Out the Barrel.[11]

Meanwhile the Major had arrived and about a dozen men (in their <u>best</u> uniforms Shambrook informed me, he himself marking the occasion by wearing new white ducks with paper label sticking out from the seat – size, no., maker, Army issue no. etc) were being drilled for his inspection by Sergeant Goddard.

The Major came up to me as I went out at the camp gate.

---

[11] A reference to 'Roll out the Barrel', a wartime drinking song popular world-wide.

'Miss Becker? I've heard so much about you from the men and seen your name up on notices about mending socks, and I'm delighted to have this opportunity of thanking you personally for all you're doing.' I mumbled something about it being my privilege.

'That's a very neat little bus you have.'

I explained, and showed the contents. 'All masculine requirements including Brylcream' I said.

'BRYLCREAM?' almost shouted the Major, but protested at my offer of a jar, though he finally accepted and paid for it!

On 6th April I went up and gave my Blythburgh lecture to about a dozen men in the recreation hut.[12] The door at the end of the room where the sheet was pinned up opened during the performance, flooding the place with light. It had to be fixed from outside with (as we found afterwards) Sergeant Podger's bed! I had tea (cold buttered toast) with the sergeants afterwards in their hut, which was quite cosy and comfortable, four of the five chairs being of my supplying!

On 17th I took my camera and Mr Birkett and another officer there temporarily, photographed all in groups, the canteen van and Ace prominent in all.

Shambrook and Boyd just had time to slip on immaculate white coats, but not the trousers to match so they skillfuly posed behind the van but came out again before the snap was taken; however they came out white all right!

One day Banham came down and asked if we'd mend his trousers – 'They're frayed here' he said, hopping on one leg to show the turn-ups.

'Take them round to Mrs Wincop' says Mummy, 'We haven't any stuff to match.'

'I can't' said Banham, 'I'm in them.'

---

[12] From the 1920s, when her parents moved to the Blythburgh hamlet of Hinton, to the end of her life, Janet Becker maintained a deep interest in the history of the village. In 1935 she published *Blythburgh. An Essay on the Village and its Church*. There is a memorial to her in the church.

21st April, 1943.

When I first went up snow was on the ground – today the bluebells are out.

29th May, 1943.

Such a commotion when I arrived in the camp this morning that I thought they were practising a paratroop invasion. There were figures stalking about between the oaks and the sentry kept shouting 'Keep down – look out – there,' and as I reached the cookhouse, Shambrook came running out with a gun at the level and jumped over the wire – and then the reason for this activity: 'We're just getting a rabbit for you, Miss Becker.'

I took up the sprays and anti-mosquito stuff; also tea and sugar for the night sentries, whose ration of both had been suddenly stopped and an issue of thick meat and vegetable soup substituted. Sergeant Goddard exclaimed 'I don't know how you think of these things, or where you get them from.' He was chaffed by Powell about first spraying himself, then the sergeant's hut etc!

Mrs Rayner told me something Banham said in the shop. At the time of the changeover of shoulder-flashes from the target to bows and arrows, I had several to put on, including two pairs for the officers. Banham gave me the wrong coat so it meant taking the pair off and transferring it. The day he was to fetch the parcel was Mummy's birthday so we went out and left the parcel with Mrs Rayner. Banham collected it when he fetched the paper and burst out to the shop 'My word, Miss Becker's a good sort - you don't know all she does for us.'

30th May, 1943.

Howlett told us tonight about the little stray dog he had in the camp, and which was said to have been seen sheep-worrying and Mr Fleming ordered it to be shot. Howlett sadly went out to dig a grave for it – the little thing played round him all the time, in and out of the hole. He then went to Swotton and said 'Will you shoot this dog for me?' and Swotton said 'Not that dog.' So he asked Boyd, and Boyd said 'I'd rather shoot Mr Fleming,' so he went to Sergeant Sinclair, 'I've never shot a dog before, and I'm not going to begin on that one.' So it was arranged it went to Chediston camp!

3rd July, 1943.

Sergeant Podger is a diplomat. Katie Lucas who is staying here wanted to go with me to see the camp. On arrival we found Sergeant Podger under the big oak talking to Alec Bird the shepherd, while Ace played with the sheepdogs.[13] 'There's a film show just beginning' he said, 'All the men are in the recreation hut – you'll stay and see the film, won't you?'

So we sat solidly in the hut till 1 p.m. watching 'Saboteur' and when we came out I had to do the selling while the men lined up with their plates for dinner at the cookhouse door.[14] Katie said she would walk on home.

Leaving the camp I met Sergeant Podger returning in the truck Tilly. 'I drove the old lady home, I thought it was a long way and too hot for her.' To Katie he had explained 'Mrs Becker will be wondering where Miss Becker is.'

Bailes turned up, having been in hospital some weeks. There is some doubt about his getting back to Henham so he came down to see everyone. 'I gave this address because I could get a travel warrant' (to a private address). He was wearing no regimental marks or searchlight flash. He said to me 'If I do come back, you'll have to do some sewing for me – I've lost all my flashes.'

---

[13] Alec H. Bird (1914-1977), born in Blythburgh. Living in The Pesthouse Cottages, Sotherton, in 1939.

[14] The film 'Saboteur', directed by Alfred Hitchcock, was released in 1942.

5th July, 1943.

There is something I should like to include. I don't know why I did not put it in its right place, except that perhaps I began this book on the lighter side.

'Does he know yet?' asked Boyd of Sergeant Podger.

'Yes, I've just sent (so and so) to relieve him on guard.'

'Found dead, wasn't she?' said someone.

'Yes, and he only came back from compassionate leave last Tuesday because she was better,' put in a third.

'The neighbours saw the blackout wasn't taken down and went in and found her lying over the side of the bed.'

'What was it?'

'Heart.'

'He's thirty – suppose she'd be about sixty.'

'Fifty-five I think he once said.'

'Who is it?' I enquired.

'Raffles – his mother died this morning.'

At that moment the subject of the conversation appeared at the cookhouse door and silence fell on all of us against our will.

Raffles was still wearing his tin hat and leather jacket he did guard in. He washed out his tea mug at the tap and then wiped it, keeping his back to us carefully all the while, and it seemed, as carefully, we avoided his gaze. I can't think why, because there wasn't one of us who wasn't very sorry for him.

On 9th July Mr Kidner judged the gardens of the Brampton, Hinton and Henham sites.[15] At the moment of writing I don't know the winner, but it was hard luck on Brampton who that morning had been visited by fifteen cows from over the fence, and had nothing to show of their vegetable garden but a ravaged and trampled plot! At Henham we turned up in time for tea. Boyd cut us cheese sandwiches – Cheese!![16] The men couldn't join our cries of enthusiasm for it as they get too much! When we had inspected the garden, we stood talking to Boyd outside the

---

[15] Stanley Kidner (1877-1961), a retired farmer, living in Reydon in 1939.

[16] The cheese ration for each civilian was 2 oz (50 g.) per week.

cookhouse in a fine drizzling rain. Mr Kidner was explaining to Boyd how they could most easily catch and kill a lamb. When Sergeant Goddard came up with his tea things for washing up, Mr Kidner was saying the bomb crater outside the cookhouse door was the very place. 'Ah,' I said, 'That crater has many uses. There was an unpopular officer here once and it was going to be his grave.'

'And it may have to be used again soon, if things go on, Miss Becker,' said Goddard. Then he went on to tell us as we stood in the rain how he had helped rush the big guns up to the Yorkshire coast after Dunkirk (there weren't any there before!) He drove them over the moors to Pickering and Whitby and Malton. Sometimes the whole convoy had to stop while the drivers and personnel wrestled with the moorland sheep asleep in the road.

10th July, 1943.

A new man Pratt on the site. He picked up a box of Gibbs Dentifrice. 'Oh,' he said 'I thought it was powder.' I said 'I can get you Eucryl or Pepsodent.' He looked a little sheepish and replied 'I meant the other sort – lady's face powder.'

'Well,' I laughed, 'I can get you some of that too –'
'I say, could you? Could you really?'
'Is she a blonde or brunette?' I asked.
'She's fair' he answered, and began to think about her.
'I'd better get a naturelle or peach shade' I said.
'Oh I don't think it matters.'
'It matters tremendously' I explained.

18th July, 1943.

I went up on Sunday because of being away. The new kitten 'Samson' was asleep on the chair in the cookhouse and would not wake up. Penny explained, 'She was on duty all night with the detachment.' As I was leaving Sergeant Podger came out of the sergeants' mess to thank me for coming up on a Sunday.

24th July, 1943.

Henham and Peasenhall tied for first prize in the gardening competition, and Chediston came second. I took up the prizes when I went with the canteen. The sergeants came up more or less in 'undress' to make their purchases. Then I said to Goddard 'Will you come and be present at the prize giving?' 'I'll fetch Sergeant Podger' he said, and returned in full dress with Sergeant Sinclair, bringing between them Sergeant Podger newly aroused from sleep, buckling belt, adjusting shirt, pulling at lanyard etc.

After the presentation to Shambrook and Boyd of ten shillings and five free double passes to Southwold cinema, they said something about putting some letters after their names, having won a prize – which was immediately taken up by all standing round.

'F.Z.S.' said Podger, amid laughter.

'That's about right' said Shambrook. 'People in zoological gardens is what looks after <u>animals</u> and feeds 'em.'

In the afternoon we went by car to Hinton and found a squad in charge of Sergeant Smith (who has replaced Sergeant Litchfield) all stripped to the waist digging and tidying up. He gave me some of the nasturtiums from their garden in exchange for apples and two cucumbers I took.

8th August, 1943.

I like going on Sundays. Everyone is, I can't say washed and dressed, but at least up and awake! This morning I took up two gallons of spray, one for Hinton and one for Henham, which I gave to Shambrook. He read out 'Kills mosquitos, flies, ants and all other pests – I'm a good mind to try some on the men, Miss Becker, I'm getting tired of them.'

One morning H.W. Reynolds told me that while he was on sentry duty about 6 a.m. he was told to keep a look-out for parachutists as some were coming down south of the site from three burning planes, making for Norwich after a raid over Germany. He didn't see any, but, I think, Sergeant Podger saw two or three of the men who had been rounded up by Battery transport. For one of them it was his first jump.

1st September, 1943.

Such a need for hair cream that I remembered what Mrs Freeman told me about her brother-in-law using medicinal paraffin, so bottled some and took it up. S.R. Smith bought some and enquired if it was alright. I said I thought so as it was pure oil only. 'What's good enough for inside is good enough for outside I should say' was his answer.[17]

18th September, 1943.

Sergeant Podger told me this morning Sergeant Goddard has departed and joined the paratroops. He volunteered in a fit of temper, not really meaning it and before he knew where he was, he was sent for.

This afternoon I walked over to Walberswick to find Chediston's new site. The village up from the ferry looks like a Russian one the Germans have evacuated – the houses that aren't in ruins are all shut up – and by ruins I don't mean bomb damage so much as the ravages of time on the jerry-built houses of the last war.[18] The ferry itself is a boat now pulled with difficulty over a swift current to and from an atrocious foreshore

---

[17] A similar product *was* in fact promoted as a hair treatment: 'Vaseline Hair Tonic', launched in the 1920s.

[18] A reflection of development known as 'Plotlands'. Cheaply-constructed and poorly-serviced dwellings were built between the wars, especially on the south coast, in south-east Essex and on its coast, and on the coast of East Anglia. Dennis Hardy and Colin Ward, *Arcadia for All. The Legacy of a Makeshift Landscape* (1984).

of brickbats and water, due to the erosion of the sea caused by the new harbour works.[19]

I followed the directions given me for finding the site, but when I came on to the common amid man-high blackberry bushes and gorse clumps I felt a bit lost, and the dirty black sand got into one's shoes as it did 30 years ago. Just then Sergeant Podger came along on his motor-bike. After a chat I gladly followed his tyre tracks to the camp, which is, as one might say, hard by the site of the old station. The sergeant received me enthusiastically, and gave me the only chair in the camp to sit on in his 'office' tent, while he sat on the table, wearing only trousers, and looking like a bronze statue of a Greek except for the ridiculous appendage of flannel 'stripes' attached to his arm with elastic! His request on being asked what they wanted most was a football.

22nd September, 1943.

This morning everyone is talking about the proposed new battle school at Frostenden and Uggeshall.[20] I found Sergeant Podger in the cookhouse, who asked if I knew where the boundaries came.

I wasn't quite sure, but I made him a good enough map sitting on the cookhouse table drawing with a finger in the air. The outcome was that the Easton Bavents new site (old Hinton Green) may be cut off – a little island of Englishmen entirely surrounded by Yanks. When Sergeant Podger heard they were to be American troops, not British, he got up and, passing his hand over his mouth, made a remark that sounded like an epigram, not only for the whole British army but the nation as well, despite the Churchill-Roosevelt propaganda. It was a case of government

---

[19] Janet Becker had known the Southwold-Walberswick chain ferry but it ceased to operate early in the war and then you had to be rowed across the river Blyth, which remains the case today. Dani Church and Ann Gander, *The Story of the Southwold-Walberswick Ferry* (2009).

[20] A battle school was an area where the infantry, in particular, could train with live ammunition. Liddiard and Sims, p.183.

proposes but man disposes. He said 'A Yank battle school? <u>It stinks already.</u>'

25th September, 1943.

This afternoon I went to Blackmoor Farm to see the Holton troop. One gets off the bus at Grey Hall Lane[21] - intriguing name when one surmises it is a corruption of Guyldhall Lane, and then finds next to the church, in the churchyard, as old a group of cottages as one could wish to see (much mauled of course) which may actually have been the Guild Hall.

I found the site, a bare field with three sleeping tents and an awning in it (the last being the cookhouse). I found only two of the personnel at home – the others were in Battery, and 'rubbling' (i.e. carrying broken bricks from Saxmundham which came by train from the Mile End Road) but these two were hosts and ambassadors in themselves. One was the cook, who apologised for his unkempt hair – 'I have a comb but nothing to look in' (so they too were promised a mirror!) I stood talking to them in the sun, while a howling north-east wind ripped the canvas and sent the smoke of the stove away over the bare fields, one side of me scorched, the other icy cold. In course of conversation one man said he hated the Americans. I thought it would be interesting to hear, so I asked why – 'Because of their uniforms and all their money, and here we are in dirty battledress for a few shillings a day.' I said what did it matter so long as the battledress was British – and what had the American soldier <u>besides</u> his pay and his uniform? Certainly not the tradition of the finest army in the world that he belonged to. Both men thought a while, the frowns erased from their foreheads as I watched, and the other said 'That's right, put like that.' The small puppy 'Panter' (born at the fall of Pantelleria)[22] - went to

---

[21] To catch a bus in the Halesworth direction, Janet Becker had to walk 1½ miles to Henham cross-roads, on the road to Beccles.

[22] Pantelleria, a small Italian island in the Mediterranean Sea, 100 km south-west of Sicily and 60 km east of the Tunisian coast. Allied forces took the island on June 11th 1943, as a prelude to the invasion of Sicily.

sleep behind the shelter of the pastry board, and I was shown round the site, and the brick paths in course of construction. 'This is the gun pit over here' said my guide as we walked over the short grass blown sideways by the wind. 'Oh,' I replied, 'I've never been allowed near a gun pit before.' He pointed to a mound of mud, 'This is where it's going to be' he explained. I saw two large flints sitting on end in the grass. 'I suppose those mark something important' I said. 'They're our goal posts' was the answer!

9th October, 1943.

I took a bunch of Michaelmas daisies up for the sergeants mess, and Bailes brought their thanks, as they were not up. 'Humf' said Shambrook – 'Wouldn't they look nice laid out with the flowers on top of them?!'

I took up also some anti-canker oil to treat the kitten's ears with. As it had been up all night with the guard, it was sleeping, and had to be brought across from the detachment hut half awake, by Bristow, who held it for me. 'You're not going to give her castor oil are you?' he enquired. Said Shambrook – 'You'd better put oil in all their ears, Miss Becker. The detachment hut never hears the breakfast whistle.'

16th October, 1943.

Caroline came in last night, having been asked the way by two soldiers. 'But' she said, 'As soon as they set off walking a "Maria" came along and picked them up!!'[23] (She meant Tilly, short for the runabout car or utility truck!)

The man in the Pioneers[24] - who helps in the cookhouse came in with a wet handkerchief, which he proceeded to dry by holding in front of the fire until Boyd took it from him and hung

---

[23] 'Black Maria', is a familiar term for a police van, typically carrying prisoners.

[24] The Pioneer Corps was formed in 1939 to provide semi-skilled labour for many different tasks.

on the dish cloth line. Until I gave him an old leather purse a week or two before he kept his money tied up in a corner of it. Sergeant Podger who was standing by the stove knew the sign: 'Going to the pictures tonight?' he asked, and received an affirmative answer.

30th October, 1943.

Pamela Freeman came up with me, and Sergeant Podger put Ace through a good many tricks for her amusement. The cat sat on a chair looking very handsome. I said 'Well, Wiggie, no one teaches you tricks,' whereupon Sergeant Podger said 'Tricks! She knows the greatest trick of all – she knows how to live comfortably without working.'

1st December, 1943.

Brough asked me to get an anniversary card for his wife on their tenth wedding day, so I said I'd do him one, and produced poetry and all:

'Ten years along the Road of Life
 Together we have gone
 And just because of you dear wife
 The sun has always shone.'

Then Shaw wanted one, for whom I wrote:

'Bright as the frost and snow
 Clear as the sky above
 Strong as the trees that grow
                So is my love!!!'[25]

The woods are bare now, and the pool where the yellow flags grew, filled with fallen leaves. It was Banham who vaulted

---

[25] Janet Becker published a volume of verse 'Flowers by Post and other verses' in 1944.

over the palings and picked me a large bunch one hot day in the summer.

6th December, 1943.

This morning Lieutenant Salmon at the front door. I had to show him into the kitchen as Mummy was only just up in the sitting room, feeling very poorly with flu. He followed me in, shutting the door. 'Just as well I should see you alone' he said mysteriously and I wondered what was coming! Major G. wanted me to know they might all be gone before Christmas, so that I could arrange about the parcels and presents accordingly.

This information, imparted while I was stirring arrowroot over the fire, set a spate of memories in motion and I wished I had kept this diary more fully and more often – that delightful tea I had after the lecture with the three sergeants in their hut off an incredibly dirty cloth but with jam tarts, and toast sodden with fat, delightful because of the spirit of hospitality in which it was offered – which even atoned for the bad manners of the fourth sergeant who took no notice of me but sat in the one easy chair (ours) and did a crossword puzzle.

The afternoon when Mr Kidner and I did the play 'Under the Counter'[26] – I wrote [There are nine blank lines here]

25th December, 1943.

I walked down to Blythburgh in the morning and returning past the camp about 1.45 there were shouts of 'Sergeant Podger, Sergeant Podger' from Sinclair, wandering round the huts, his hands to his mouth. A little further on I met Sergeant Podger on a bicycle coming from the village. 'Ah' I said, 'This accounts for the cries for Sergeant Podger coming from the wood.' We

---

[26] Under the Counter: things that are bought secretly and illegally. The Victoria and Albert Museum Theatre and Performance Enquiry Service was unable to identify the play. It could have been for amateurs only. However, a 50-minute play with this title was written for Cicely Courtneidge and broadcast on the Light Programme on 2 September 1946. (British Newspaper Archive, Derby Free Press, 2 September 1946). A musical comedy version ran for two years in London at the end of the war.

exchanged a few words and pleasantries and then the smiles faded from his face and he looked straight at me: 'They sounded all right, didn't they?' he exclaimed, anxious as any nanny whose charges are out of sight. I was able to assure him, and it transpired afterwards, they were waiting for him to help carve the turkey.

1st January, 1944.

Sergeant Podger says the only difference between A.B.I. (Assistant Battle Instructor) Sinclair and Ace is that Ace doesn't have to pretend to work. Sinclair was there, of course, and had some good rejoinder which I've forgotten.

26th February, 1944.

The sign posts are being replaced, and the old milestone outside the camp has reappeared from under its mound of soil and thatch of turf. [27]
In camp, quite good spirits. Reed (the new cook) was teasing S.R. Smith about snoring so loud he didn't know if it was the diesel or not.[28]
Sergeant Sinclair told me that when they play football in the evenings Ace goes so wild he has to be tied up with Sergeant Sinclair's braces!

11th March, 1944.

I went to tea with the Wrentham site this afternoon by invitation of Sergeant Smith who said when last I went (walking against a snowstorm all the way from the bus, carrying a big pot of flowering daffodils that acted like a sail) that if only I could stay a little longer I could have tea with them.

---

[27] Road signs were removed at the start of the war because of their possible use to an invading force. They were replaced once invasion was no longer a serious threat.

[28] The Lister JP4 diesel engine used to generate power for the searchlight.

As I approached the camp, the new officers, Mr Panter (nicknamed Pauser) and Atkinson passed me in the Tilly. When I told them where I was going they said 'So <u>that</u> accounts for the tremendous clearing up and sweeping and scrubbing that was going on when we left – we wondered ….'

I sat and listened to the football match on the wireless till tea was 'served' – a large dixie full of pancakes (with <u>real</u> lemon juice, as I discovered on seeing pips on Matthew's plate, who sat next to me) and a pint mug of tea. Sergeant Smith sat at the head of the table on my right. I discovered he came from Rotherham but he didn't know Wrentham Street, only Reydon Road. After tea and the sharing out of my cake, which turned out to be really rather a good one, I gave them a little demonstration of lino-block printing and got rather black doing it. Before I could make more than two or three ineffective dabs at my fingers with wet blotting paper and water out of the dish we wetted the paper in, Banham had sprung from the living hut into the sleeping compartment, and fetched his own (damp) towel and pink soap. Then he rushed outside and returned with an enormous round galvanised bath full of hot water! I got a lift back in the ration lorry with Pratt.

15th March, 1944.

Sergeant Podger was telling me about the crash of a bomber at Benacre, when men of the Wrentham site got five dead bodies out of a pond which has engulfed the plane – and offered to show me some 'Perspex' he had picked up.[29] He took me into the office and produced a huge lump of glassy substance he told me was made of milk 'and something.' He is making little crosses and rings out of it.[30] Had I any little glass beads? I said yes, and

---

[29] On 13th March 1944 a B-24 Liberator bomber from Hardwick, Norfolk, fell out of control from a gathering formation, and crashed at Walnut Tree Farm. Four of the crew bailed out and survived.

[30] Perspex is a transparent acrylic material, Polymethyl Methacrylate, often recovered from the canopies of crashed aircraft and easily moulded into rings and other jewellery.

if I gave them to him I would like a little ring if he'd make me one. 'I'd be very pleased to' he said. I never got it.

Outside he suddenly stopped and picked up a long black strip of 'paper', dropped by the Jerries last night.[31] He said he couldn't tell me what exactly it did, as the Germans would like to know just how much it interfered with our radio location, but he said I should find it all on the front page of the Daily Express![32]

From the cookhouse window we watched tits flitting about round the canteen tray, and when I came out there were neat little holes pecked in the buns!

24th March, 1944.

Penny came down tonight and said Pratt left this morning, to re-join Heavy Artillery. Sorry about this, as he was such a cheerful efficient person, and so <u>obliging</u> in taking my messages and parcels round the sites, and he never passed one in the ration lorry without a waved salute.

29th March, 1944.

I was in the baker's shop getting the cakes when two Liberators crashed and fell in the park.[33] First there were two big explosions (the bombs falling as the planes disintegrated) and then the whine and scrape of machinery gone wrong. Peggy Townsend came rushing back from the bakehouse. 'There's one

---

[31] Large quantities of aluminised paper strips, known as 'Window', were dropped by the RAF from 1943 onwards to confuse enemy radar systems. The Luftwaffe responded in kind.

[32] The Daily Express was the biggest-selling daily newspaper with a circulation that peaked at four million in the 1940s. It had a reputation for scoops, many attributable to its investigative defence correspondent Chapman Pincher, who supplied the paper with intelligence even while serving in the army during the war.

[33] Two B-24 Liberator bombers from Hardwick, Norfolk, collided over Henham and fell in the park. Various numbers have been published for the casualties. Post-war research indicates that sixteen of the nineteen crew died. A further six rescuers were killed and over thirty injured when a bomb in one of the aircraft exploded. There is a memorial in the park.

of them double-tailed planes falling to pieces in the air.' By the time I got outside with the tray of cakes there was nothing to be seen but two columns of black smoke over the Henham woods. As I passed the school another explosion took place. As I turned into the camp a Jeep followed me, and to my surprise Pedley got out – his mouth covered in blood. 'They nearly got me' he managed to say, and sought a dry place in his handkerchief. It appeared he was doing 30-40 mph on the motor-bike when a Yank lorry overtook him. The driver seeing an airman's boot by the side of the road, pulled up dead in his tracks and Padley had no choice but to go slap into the lorry's tail board. He might have been killed – as it was his front teeth were either broken or loosened. Talking we reached the cookhouse and he went in before me because I was parking the canteen. His suppressed groan was taken by Boyd as being a remark on the general situation – smoke belching up over the trees – all the men on the site away to the wreckage and all the windows blown out of the Hall. But as I entered, he saw the blood stains on Pedley's overall, hands and face. Pedley told the story. We exclaimed together 'Sit down, you ought to sit down,' and I on one side of him and he on the other, we were going to assist him to a chair, but he broke away from us. 'I must spit' he said and went outside, returning, joined by the first of the men, now drifting back across the park. 'Whatever's the matter with you' they asked, and Pedley retold his tale again.

'Did you see the tail come off?' someone asked me, sitting on the table, 'And then the wings - <u>Coo</u> -.'

'No,' I said 'I never see anything like that – I'm never in the right place at the right time.' I was standing with my back to the window, Boyd in front of me, laughing at this remark when he suddenly made a gesture, and I wheeled round to see a 2000-pound bomb go up with the same volumes of smoke and flashes of fire as one sees in photographs, but I cannot remember hearing any <u>noise</u>. We all tumbled out of the cookhouse and stood watching and discussing it, when suddenly what <u>seemed</u> like a full two minutes after there was a whirring sound like the winging of some great bird. Instinctively we all ducked – it was the strangest feeling having one's body forcibly pulled towards the ground. It was just as if someone put a hand on the back of one's neck and pushed. The whizzing grew louder and then stopped, as a big piece of shrapnel landed among the wild hyacinth leaves on the furthest side of the cookhouse.

More men were now coming up, each with a fresh experience. Bailes and T.W. Smith brought a large bit of metal with them. It had fallen beside them just as Smith was saying 'There's a bird flying round.'

Interesting the way the commotion took people …. One man who usually hasn't half a dozen words a week for me started describing a garden he made at his London home, and how could he get tomato plants for a garden he was making in the camp. Boyd, often tired or disgruntled, was almost hysterical with amusement that the Hall windows were shattered, and someone else often quite rude in the very limited scope that canteen purchasing affords him, started saying 'please' and 'thank you' (and has kept up pleasantries not to say conversation ever since 29.4.44).

Easter Sunday, 9th April 1944.

Visited Hinton in a downpour of Spring rain. The cook requested flowers for his sick wife. The others stood around in a respectful circle and awed silence! Said the cook by way of explanation, 'You see, Miss, you're the only lady we ever see here. There is another one, lives in a farm two miles over there,' pointing where the sun was breaking through a haze of green across the fields, 'but she never comes to the camp.'

24th June, 1944.

I went on the ration lorry to Saxmundham this morning on way to the Grays.[34] Returning in the evening to go back by train

---

[34] Old friends at Benhall Cottage, Benhall Green. Artist John Gray (1869-1951) and his wife Dulabella (nee Gooch, 1876-1949).

I met all the men who had been at Battery sports.[35] Bert
Reynolds and Pedley were on my side of the pavement and asked
how I was getting back. Pedley said I should not risk getting a lift
from Halesworth and that a lorry was returning in an hour. Why
not go along with them. 'But I shall be in the way' I said. Pedley
looked me full in the face. 'Miss Becker,' he said, 'You're not in
the way when you come with the canteen, are you?'

July, 1944.

　　　Widdie, alias onetime Samson, the kitten, came into the
cookhouse this morning with a most marked matronly waddle. I
was alone with Boyd so I said 'So she wasn't a Samson after all.'
'She'll be all right' he began, 'She'll be all right. Bristow's looking
after her. He's never done seeing to her.'

　　　Later, seven kittens were born under the floor of
Detachment's sleeping hut. They feared the draught for her, so
took up the floor boards and lifted Widdie and the kittens out,
putting her in a box in a pen, roofed with corrugated iron. At 11
p.m. there was a scratching at the door and Widdie walked in
with a kitten in her mouth which she laid on the centre of the
floor and went back for the next ……. She now lives in
Detachment hut with two fine kits.

Copy of letter. 13th September, 1944.

Dear Sergeant Podger,

　　　Since the takings of the WVS canteen have been steadily
falling for several weeks past I have been thinking that its services
were no longer really wanted. Sergeant Spilman explained that
battery canteen supplies were now delivered on Saturdays so I cut
out one visit and now I find the Salvation Army also visits twice a
week so my canteen is hardly necessary any more.

---

[35] The East Suffolk line runs from Ipswich to Lowestoft. The station for Wangford is Halesworth.

I shall be pleased to carry on with the sock-darning if wanted and if it can be arranged for them to be brought and fetched at newspaper time on Wednesdays and Saturdays.

Yours sincerely
M.J. Becker
(I had been up 175 times)

21ˢᵗ October, 1944.

    I visited Walberswick site and found Sergeant Smith and Shambrook had become expert cake makers. The whole camp has had to be up all night long for several nights working the searchlight in a circle to signal our aircraft off a machine [gun?] nest.[36] So Smith and Shambrook in their midnight break have been in the habit of returning to the cookhouse <u>in their tin hats</u> and making sponges with mock cream fillings!

****

CORNER SHOP

The lady at the corner shop
Sells everything –
From saucepans to a lollipop
From cabbages to string

But when in war supplies would drop -
'Nothing for miles'
She stood inside her empty shop
And gave away her smiles.

M. Janet Becker 1947

****

---

[36] The use of the searchlight to assist allied aircraft.

Appendix

Beccles and Bungay Journal Saturday, August 7th 1943.

IN TOWN and VILLAGE

Searchlight Men's Interest in 'Dig for Victory' Campaign

Quite a lot of interest in the Government's 'Dig for Victory' campaign has been aroused among the men serving in searchlight units in one district of East Anglia as the result of the efforts of Miss M. Janet Becker of Wangford. Each site has a good-sized garden on which a varying proportion of the men work in their spare time. In March, Miss Becker asked Mr. Stanley Kidner, a well-known figure in the farming world, to come along to the particular area in July and judge five gardens. They went round three of them together, and Mr Kidner did the other two. His report and awards have just come along. Telling me about the tour, Miss Becker said it was real hard luck on one site that it should have been visited a few hours before their arrival by a herd of cows from an adjoining meadow. 'They ravaged the vegetable patch from end to end so that we could not distinguish between the different plants' she remarked. 'However, the men at this site had laid out the piece of ground round its searchlight in four triangular beds with cinder and brick paths, so they picked up their points on lay-out.' Mr Kidner reported that he was much impressed by the variety of vegetables grown and the amount of care and work expended in their cultivation. Several of the paths between and round the plots were of 'crazy' pattern. Two sites tied for first prize. One received cash and free passes to the local cinema and the other a couple of hundred cigarettes. The prize of a hundred cigarettes went to the site gaining fourteen points out of a possible twenty. To each of the five camps was given a trophy shield. Three of these had been designed and painted by Gunner

L. Howlett and Craftsman W. G. Penny, who are attached to a searchlight post served by Miss Becker's mobile canteen.

*   *   *

Miss Becker gave me some interesting information concerning this canteen and the good work she is able to do with it. Actually it is in the form of a box-trailer for a pedal cycle. Since December she has taken it twice a week into the countryside with a good load of cigarettes, hot buns, chocolates, razor blades and various other things likely to be in demand by service men. 'My boast is that no man has ever asked me for a razor blade in vain' Miss Becker remarked. On her return home she brings their mending which she takes back to them on the occasion of her next tour. Not long ago she had many battledress blouses and tunics to sew. With the assistance of a W.V.S. friend, Mrs. Hilda Freeman, 'without whose unstinted help and unfailing cooperation I should never get through my undertakings.' Miss Becker has just completed a 1400-piece patchwork quilt, an order for her Services fund. Some time ago she was able to augment this fund by making and selling Valentines to members of the Forces and also in two London shops. These were charming pieces of work being in the form of pink silk hearts stuffed with pot-pourri and pierced with arrows of silver paper.

*   *   *

[The conclusion of this article is missing]

Suggestions for further reading

Janet Becker's published work:

Notes on the Church and Village of Wenhaston (1923)

Rochester Bridge: 1387-1856. A History of its early years compiled from the Wardens' accounts (1930)

Blythburgh. An Essay on the Village and the Church (1935)

Ploughshare into Pylon (1939)

Flowers by Post (1944)

Monumental Art as a Mirror to the Past. Address to the Friends of Lincoln Minster (1947)

Story of Southwold (Editor) (1948)

Sutherland House and Sole Bay (1949)

The Thirsty Oak (USA, 1950), published in England as *David without Jonathan* (1951)

****

R. Douglas Brown, *East Anglia 1939 to 1945* (In seven volumes, 1980-1994)

David E. Johnson, *East Anglia at War* (1992)

Robert Liddiard and David Sims, *A Guide to Second World War Archaeology in Suffolk* (2014)

> *Guide 1: Lowestoft to Southwold*
>
> *Guide 2: Walberswick to Aldeburgh*
>
> *Guide 3: Orford to Felixstowe*
>
> *Guide 4: Stop Lines*

Robert Liddiard and David Sims, *A Very Dangerous Locality. The Landscape of the Suffolk Sandlings in the Second World War* (2018)

David Shirreff and Arthur Sharman, eds, *Suffolk Memories. Stories of Walberswick and Blythburgh people during World War II* (1998)

Arthur Sharman and Patricia Wythe, eds, *Further Suffolk Memories. More stories of Walberswick and Blythburgh people during World War II* (2001)

David Thompson, *Becker* (2002)

* * * * * * * * * * * * * * * * * * * *

Hangar